Poetry Pleasures

All In Rhyme

By

Sandra Stoner-Mitchell

CONTENTS

~~TO MY HUSBAND GRAHAM~~

For your constant support and faith in me

The Sad Piano ©

The sad piano, once so proud, stood bravely by the door;
its feet were coated thick with dust that rose up from the floor.
In days, now passed, the row of shiny blacks and pearly whites,
would dance away as fingers played the keys throughout the night.

Now left alone to waste away, no one there left to care,
it sadly stands and hopes one day someone will see it there.
It longed to play again the music deep inside its soul,
it still had spirit waiting for someone to make it whole.

To feel the touch of fingers' play as people danced around
To see the joy on faces as they listened to its sound
To feel the beat inside its heart, to hear its music sing
To be a part of someone's life would mean just everything.

But now the room was empty, people gone, the home had died,
They'd left their old piano here, like scrap, just cast aside.
It wondered if this was the end, alone forevermore;
and then a little girl came singing through the open door.

She danced into the centre of the dusty, empty place,
when suddenly she saw it, and a smile lit up her face.
The sad piano waited, and it looked into her eyes
and saw a love so special, it was taken by surprise.

The little girl walked over, and her hands caressed its keys,
her fingers then began to move; she played a tune with ease.
Her parents came in laughing, and it heard them turn and say,
'We'd like to buy this house, but that piano has to stay.'

At last the old piano's music came alive once more
He'd always play sweet music that the young girl would adore

~~oOo~~

A Tiny Tear ©

This blush pink rose is all that's left to see
a tiny bud once glazed with morning's dew
a small reminder of what used be
and of the love she'll always hold for you

***

The bud lies gently in her trembling hand
it once was woven in her wedding spray
She closed her eyes … she couldn't understand
how could a life so good end in this way?

***

She can remember everything from when
you came home early and took her outside
she didn't want to hear those words…and then
you held her in your arms as you both cried

***

The sun sets low and turns the ocean pink
the colour of this rose she sends to you
she looked towards the orb and watched it sink
then threw the rose into its golden hue

A tiny tear falls down onto her lips
she feels the trace of your sweet fingertips

~~oOo~~

Turned to Stone ©

The sun blazed down to boil the day,
the cold moon froze the night,
the air was stifled by the rays, a daily, searing blight.
The people who were still alive,
found moving hard to bear,
they sat around all comatose; 'twas hard to breath this air.

***

One day, a drifter wandered into
town and looked around--
he walked into the nearest bar—the only one in town.
The men looked up, surprised to see
this stranger come inside;
he stared at them through tortured eyes,
his pain he couldn't hide.

***

He had a drink, a whiskey neat, and then said, 'Same again.'
he drank to take away the sights and to remove the pain.
He turned around and then he said, 'I have a tale to tell
about a world that we once had but now has gone to hell.

'I've been around the globe to see
an Earth once plush and green,
where rivers flowed, and forests grew, some sights I'd never seen.

When stars came out, the moon was bright,
as night-time hid the blue,
where life was good, and all had hope,
and dreams were coming true.

'But greed came by to squeeze the world,
we took all that we could;
The more we seized, and less we gave,
we never understood—

to raze the trees, we take the lungs
that clean the air we breathe,
And now they're gone, there's nothing left
our children to bequeath.

We raped our planet ruthlessly,
we stripped her to the bone,
we broke the heart of Mother Earth,
and now she's turned to stone.'

~~o~~

He Opened Up His Eyes ©

He closed his eyes, then breathed in deeply as he sighed;
the scent of salty seas invading senses--
long ago denied.
What message had the Spirits of his people to impart?
His mind wandered…waiting…

Was that sound the sea-gulls screeching loudly in the sky?
Not from any memory of his did he recall…but then--
could it be the sound of eagles so far distant as to fall
upon his hearing, gently reminiscing days that fly,
in ever spinning eons passing by.

With eyes still closed; did he hear wings? Or fins of fish
that leap out of the waters, gasping wide,
relinquishing their freedom to the ever-spawning tide.

He listened to the sounds of life abounding all around…
he frowned, his heart sore—stricken to the core

knowing this reality
was, in its entirety, a time so long before…

… the white man.

Then suddenly 'twas clear, the reason he was here
brought before the spirits on his own.
Up on the mountain high, with the eagles in the sky
brought together some normality
of family and home.

His eyes, eager now to open
as the breeze, bringing far-off laughter that in turn
would lift his lips…
he traced with fingertips—then suddenly he realized—

that everything he had despised had made him now the man he had
become.
He'd turned what was, into what is.

He opened up his eyes.

~~oOo~~

Music Man ©

Although he'd been a friend for years,
we never knew his name;
the month he came to visit us, had always been the same.
And with his old umbrella opened up and never down,
we relished his arrival; he brought music to our town.

We all called him our 'Music Man'
he brought us joy each year;
the town would buzz with merriment,
the moment he was here.

He made amazing music as he wandered through the day,
creating joy in everyone he met along the way
By showing children that to play an instrument is fun he taught them
all that music was a gift for everyone.

We all called him our 'Music Man'
he brightened up our town;
he'd put a smile upon our face,
when we were feeling down.

But this year was so different,
when no music came our way;
we told each other, he's just late, and waited every day.
Then when his time had long passed by,
so we all understood,
the day we'd hoped would never come…
our friend had gone for good.

We still call him our 'Music Man'
he sends his melody,
by raining notes down on us with
angelic harmony.

~~oOo~~

The Death of Paper Books ©

***

She stood there in the centre of the room and looked around;
her eyes the size of saucers focused on the things they'd found.
'What are all these?' she asked her granddad, reaching out in awe
to touch the books upon the shelves. 'What was this building for?'

***

Her granddad smiled, although his eyes were sad as he recalled
these paper books, that long ago, had kept him so enthralled.
How dearly he had loved their smell…the sight of pages' bound
in leather and in paperback; but now so rarely found.

***

He tried explaining to the child in words she'd understand,
the joy of holding books and feeling pages in your hand.
'These buildings were called libraries,' he whispered reverently.
'And all the shelves were packed with books for us to read for free.

***

16

'As children we would come from school to find something to read;
a good adventure story as each one would sow its seed.
One day I'd be a cowboy, or stop villains rob the bank,
or I would be the hero saving folk from ships that sank!'

***

The little girl then giggled, and said, 'Granddad, you are fun.
These books must be so heavy, just a few would weigh a ton!
While I can hold a thousand books here in my tiny hand,
upon my Tablet, and no trees were taken from the land.'

***

Her granddad sighed, 'Perhaps you're right, but I like paper best!'
he told her most defiantly while pumping out his chest.

***

~~oOo~~

The Gate ©

The gate was old and broken
leading nowhere anymore,
the path, now gone, once led up to
a warm and welcome door.

***

What was an English country garden,
soon became a field,
and though the house had gone
the gate, alone, refused to yield

****

Once children played there happily,
from dawn till early dusk,
in gardens full of shrubs and plants
exuding fragrant musk.

***

Where ladies played croquet on lawns,
and tennis on hard ground;
while most had gone and more would go—
the gate was still around.

***

The ocean had been coming
closer slowly now for years,
while gentry sought to save their homes,
it ended all in tears.

***

And, gradually, the seas
continued taking
back the land
as battered cliffs gave up the fight
against the oceans hand.

***

But, through it all the gate still stood,
beat-up beyond repair;
a sentinel for what had been
and was no longer there.

~~oOo~~

Happy Days ©

I found this picture yesterday –
'ere, take a look and see.
Remember old Pa Jones?
He took this snap of you and me.
Cor blimey, didn't we 'ave fun,
just sat there on the sand,
pretendin' we was toffs, and lived a life so bloomin' grand.

We ate some whelks and winkles
from a frayed old paper cup…
We 'ad to use the safety pins
that 'eld me knickers up,
to pull the winkles from their shells;
oh boy, we 'ad a laugh.
If the kids 'ad seen us, they'd a thought us both were daft.

Remember you went paddlin'
with your pants rolled to yer knees?
You wanted me to come in
but I said me toes would freeze!
You messed around so much
you didn't see that big wave come
It was so high the bloomin' thing
then flicked you on yer bum!

I laughed so 'ard; you tried to stand,
then down you went again.
In stitches, I was laughin'
that I got a bloomin' pain!
Soaked you were, through to your butt,
I'll not forget that day.
But, now I come to think on it …
that's when you stomped away!

Okay, okay, I'm sorry,
but you would've laughed at me,
if I'd a been the one that 'ad been dunked there in the sea.
Alright! I'll put the snap away;
just what is wrong with you?
There ya go, I've torn it up – you bloomin' mis'ry moo!

~~oOo~~

Spider Webs (an acrostic)©

Spiders webs are works of art
Produced with care each perfect part
In circles shaped with silver threads
Draped over trees and flower beds
Each silken line holds strong and true
Receiving flies and insects too

When moving home the spiders then
Eat up their webs and start again
Born master craftsmen everyone
Spinning their webs are jobs well done.

~~oOo~~

Sunset ©

The sky is tinged with splendid shades
of bronze and Aztec gold,
And when the sun drops through the clouds,
so night skies soon unfold.
A hush occurs as all the birds
tuck heads beneath their wings,
And soothed to sleep by gentle serenades the evening brings.

As trees receive the day's last glow
upon their leaves of green,
the sun slips further to bequeath
a subtle golden sheen.
And by the time this orb has set,
and gone till dawn is due,
so all will rest, and be refreshed when day starts out anew.

~~oOo~~

The Light of Hope ©

The sea was rough; the waves were high and grey,
the sailors prayed to God to show the way
to safer, calmer seas so they might be
allowed to sail back home to family.
But every toss the ship was thrown,
so, sailors thought they were alone.
They heard the hull, they heard it moan
as it tried hard to take them home.

The sailors thought their prayers had gone unheard,
that in the storm the tide took every word
and tossed them to the bottom of the sea …
And that is where they knew they'd all soon be.
And then a shout came from the nest,
a light they'd spied along the crest
was flashing on and off to show the way …
It was His lighthouse come to save the day.

~~oOo~~

Wild Flowers ©

He opens his umbrella over rambling flower-beds,
and sits there when the noon-day sun
reclines just overhead—
he'll take his pad and pencils out, and sketch till end of day,
then when the sun sets gracefully, he'll pack it all away.

He is the only artist from a thousand painters known
who draws the way the landscape is,
the way it should be shown.
His creativity brings life and purpose to the fore,
by using nature's pigments to reflect the inner core

He's done this now for many years, he'll do it till he dies.
He'll watch the landscape changing
underneath the shifting skies,
then paint it on his canvas so that everyone can see
the beauty that is all around and given to us free.

While Nature creates images to please us every day,
the artist does it equally but in a different way.

~~oOo~~

That Little Piece ©

When I was just a child of four,
my mother gave to me
a picture box of pieces,
and I thought, what could they be?

***

Each little piece a different shape,
with bits of pictures on,
and then my mother told me
I must find where they belong.

***

With tongue jammed tight between my teeth
I concentrated hard,
And picked up every little piece
cut from a picture card.

***

I tried to make the pieces
join together every day,
I thumped and pushed but in the end,
I just went out to play.

***

Each year I had another
and each time I struggled too,
Until one year I mastered it
and I knew what to do.

***

'Twas then my mother told me
that real life is just like this,
With patience and persistence,
you'll enjoy a life of bliss.

***

So, if an opportunity
comes knocking on your door,
It might just be that perfect fit
that you've been looking for.

~~oOo~~

Born with Music in His Soul ©

With his guitar and violin
both always close at hand,
this man will play sweet melodies,
for all throughout the land.

And when the people flock around,
I've often heard them say,
'We always hear the angels sing
each time he starts to play'.

For there's an air about him
when he picks up his guitar,
an aura of divinity,
you'll feel it from afar.

Some say that he was born
with music deep within his soul,
and he has sworn to share his gift;
to please God is his goal.

So if you listen carefully,
to whispers in the breeze,
you might just hear the sound of music
rustling through the leaves.

for when he strums his old guitar
or strokes his violin,
The breeze comes by and plucks it high
to carry it within.

~~oOo~~

The Journey ©

'Twas the twenty-fourth September in eighteen-ninety-two,
I'd journeyed on a steam train in my quest to be with you.
It was a fearsome venture for a lady on her own,
to travel through uncharted lands so very far from home.

I'd heard about such frightful things
that happened on a train,
and though I'd tried to still my heart,
my efforts were in vain.

The deeper into savage land, the more concerned was I
of reaching you, my one true love—
I'd feared that I might die.

I'd heard the whistle loud and clear,
I'd heard some shooting too,
And, looking out the window,
I did not know what to do.

I saw so many Indians, with paint on every face,
and though the train was going fast,
their horses had kept pace.

The ladies had been screaming
when the train was slowing down,
but I'd been feared to silence wishing I was back in town.
My parents had desired for me to wait until you came,
but I'd been so determined, I had only me to blame.

The Indians had come on board,
and they killed every man.
The women, they would take away
but shoot them if they ran--
while I'd sat very quietly and tried to hide from view--
just hoping they'd not see me there, was all that I could do.

And then I'd heard the cavalry
come charging from the rear;
the Indians would not give up,
they made that very clear.
The cavalry fought hard and long, the Indians did too,
and when it was all over, it was then that I saw you.

I'd called your name out loudly,
and you came and held me tight.
And now it seems so long ago as I sit here this night,
describing to our grandchildren how you had rescued me.
My hero, and my soul mate, I am yours eternally.

~~oOo~~

The Autumn Lady ©

I'm going to tell a story of a lady dressed in gold
A lady who prepares the land against the Winter cold
Once Summer starts to pack away
the warm rays of the sun
So, Lady Autumn knows her busy time has just begun

She's not a friend of Winter,
and with Summer she's no fan
since both are bitter enemies and argue when they can
The Summer Sun would try to stay
and thaw out Winter's frost
whose icy fingers sought to freeze the Sun at any cost

The war was such that for a while
the Winter froze the Earth
The ice age lasted eons meaning life could not give birth
But then the Sun grew stronger
and came charging back again
And dried the Earth till parched
and needing life supporting rain

And so it was the Autumn Lady came between the two,
and with the Spring she sought to bring
back life on Earth anew
Now once the Summer Sun has gone,
she'll put the plants to bed
and blanket them with falling leaves
of golds and blazing reds

The Autumn Lady paints the Earth
with gold and bronze displays
which brightens up the land
and gives us freshly scented days

~~oOo~~

The Storm ©

The waves were rolling higher
than the mast upon the boat
The Captain shouted orders as
they tried to stay afloat

The wind was screaming loud as if it was the devil's wail
It tore and clawed the rigging that was holding up the sail

The bow was lifted up
which put the keel under duress
It groaned and shrieked and shuddered
as if dying in distress

As seamen fought to save themselves
against the raging squall
They heard a sudden sound
which was familiar to them all

The men all looked across the waves
and gliding near the tide
They saw two sea-gulls flying,
and the gale start to subside.

The sea-gulls are God's messengers,
and this they understand
He sent them there to tell the men
they were now close to land

With faith, the turmoil of the sea can soon become a pond
As God will walk beside you in this life and then beyond

~~oOo~~

When Rain Obscures the Light ©

He wanders through the city streets when rain obscures the light
His eyes are lowered, collar up, his face is out of sight
The shadows of the people passing by are unaware
They do not know this enigmatic man is even there

His heart was taken long ago, she stole it with a kiss
He'd never known such happiness, his waking hours bliss
She'd given him the joy of life, the laughter and the fun
And when the sky was overcast, her smile brought out the sun

Until that day when he woke up to grey clouds in the sky
His love had gone away, he knew not where, or even why
He's searched the whole world over, and he'll search for ever more
Until she's in his arms again, his heart's a shrivelled core.

He wanders through the city streets when rain obscures the light,
A broken shell of who he was, he disappears from sight.

I'll Be Back in a While ©

My memory has taken a trip to a place
That tickles the tips of my lips on my face,
Where goblins a hobbling are messing around
To a mystical, magical, musical sound.

My memories are muddled and fuddled...who cares?
Just mingling and tingling with life unawares,
Where time can go slowly and stop for a while
To capture the magic that brings on a smile.

My memories are jiggling and wiggling around
To take me to places no other has found,
Where pixies play Dixie and elves have a ball,
Delighting in feathers that flutter and fall.

Today didn't happen so why should I care?
Tomorrow? Who knows? I might not be there!
But yesterday beckons me back with a smile,
So sorry, I'm gone...I'll be back in a while.

~~oOo~~

She Walked with God ©

***

Her silver hair was flecked with gold,
her eyes were emerald green,
her mind was filled with memories
of good things she had seen.

***

She had a tranquil aura—
a soft gentleness so rare,
and emanated love and joy
to everybody there.

***

We all sat very quietly,
expectant and beguiled,
while she told stories of her trips
to every spellbound child..

***

She'd travelled far when she was young
to spread God's holy word,
and went to places no one knew
with names we'd never heard.

***

She'd been across the ocean,
and trekked many jungles too,
brought Jesus to the children,
made them see the world anew.

***

She told us tales of those she'd met,
how humbled she had been,
by all the kindness she'd been shown
and wonders she had seen.

***

We saw the glow shine in her eyes,
the soft smile on her face--
and we knew as we looked at her—
she walked in God's embrace.

~~oOo~~

The Strike ©

The woman looked around the room—
what could she burn today?
There was no coal, no logs around,
to keep the chill at bay.

Her children huddled up real
close to share their body heat;
their clothes were old and full of holes,
they'd no shoes for their feet.

The strike had taken everything;
they could not pay the rent.
No food to feed the little ones,
the money was all spent.

The Union said, 'It won't take long,
the gentry will soon pay.'
But that was many months ago,
and neither would give way.

She'd burned the chairs; the table too,
the wooden beds were next.
How could the gentry be so cruel?
It left her so perplexed.

Those up the hill had fancy homes
and food upon their plate,
while she could not recall at all,
the last good meal they ate.

The woman will go out today,
her pride could not intrude,
she'll pound the doors of those with wealth
and beg for scraps of food.

But sure, as not, she will come home
without a crust of bread;
another day she'll cry inside...
her children won't be fed.

The union called a meeting
for its members to hold fast
'We've come this far, we can't give in;
their arrogance can't last.

So, join with me and let them know,
we're made of sterner stuff!'
The men agreed, but those at home
had simply had enough.

Around this time the woman found
her youngest child had died,
she screamed out loud, her neighbours'
came and with the woman cried.

>>

'Enough's enough,' the woman sobbed,
'no more can we go on.'
The women called a meeting
for a plan to act upon.

'We'll go together,' they agreed.
'No longer can we wait,
the rich will hear our voices now!'
Their hearts were filled with hate.

The woman picked her dead child up,
and marched straight out the door.
Her child did not deserve to die
so young for being poor.

The women marched right up the hill,
determined now to show
those ladies in their fancy homes,
some things they ought to know.

The mother with her poor dead child,
would lead them in this fight,
She planned to touch their consciences,
and vowed they'd make things right.

The group was stood outside the house—
they'd never been so near.
To see the type of wealth they had
was hideously clear.

Before they could pound on the door,
the butler flung it wide,
it didn't bother him at all
to see a child had died.

He told them all to leave at once,
or he would call the law.
'You riff-raff are not welcome here.'
He turned to close the door.

But then a voice behind him asked, '
Has someone come to call?'
The butler answered, 'No, Madam—
there's no one here at all.'

The lady came up to the door,
and saw the crowd outside,
and then she spied the mother
who held close the child that died

She clutched her heart and felt quite faint,
the butler held her arm,
He turned to her and falsely said,
'They've come to do you harm.'

The woman with the child then cried,
'I'll beg, for pity's sake!
We only want to feed our babes,
what difference could it make

to all you rich and wealthy folk,
to pay men what they're worth?'
'The difference is' the butler said,
it comes down to your birth.'

Another day, another night,
how long could this strike last?
And then one day a man appeared,
he said the time had passed.

>>

'The pits will close unless you men
go back to work today,
and if you do, you'll have a raise,
two shillings in your pay.'

The women turned towards their men,
and told them to agree;
they'd lost too much and must accept,
to end this misery.

The woman who had lost her child said,
'If you don't...I'll leave.
The strain has been too much to bear,
I need some time to grieve.'

And so the men went back to work,
it seemed no side had won.
They thought it would be over quick—
when first it had begun.

But food is on the children's plate;
there's coal for burning, too,
and owners paying men their worth,
for what they have to do.

~~oOo~~

I'm Sorry Dear…

How many times we must have met;
although this mind of mine regrets
there are occasions I forget
how many times we must have met.

I do remember long ago
you were someone I used to know,
but though my mind will ebb and flow
I do remember long ago.

Your name, my dear, escapes my mind;
I try to think, but life's unkind.
I'm getting old, too old to find
your name, my dear, escapes my mind.

How many times we must have met—
I'm sorry dear...but I forget...

~~oOo~

Hitching a Ride ©

I'm standing by the motorway,
the traffic's going fast
I show a thumb and hope someone
will stop and not go past
I'll hitch a lift to somewhere
in fact anywhere will do
As long as it's at least a hundred thousand miles from you

***

I thought of you my soul-mate—
as my bright and shining star
My universe my everything,
for you I'd travel far
But then I saw you with my friend,
wrapped in each other's arms
She found it easy to succumb to your seductive charms

***

I must have shed a million tears,
before I understood
You are a rat who loves the chase
and then you're gone for good
I read the words of love you wrote
to fill me with desire
Then shed a tear once more before I threw it on the fire

***

I guess it was bad luck I found
a toe-rag such as you
Good fortune wasn't smiling down
upon the card I drew
In subtle ways you told me
that you wouldn't stay around
But I just didn't listen I believed our love was sound

***

And now my battered heart needs time to heal and then move on
I'll hitch a ride and won't be back until I know you've gone

The Ice Man

3000 BC

The new sky shimmered with a crystalline blush,
That gave distant mountains an ethereal hush.
The man who stood watching, not knowing the cause,
Just relished the moment and took time to pause.

The mountain was calling, demanding he go,
Before the arrival of blizzards of snow.
The other side beckoned and time wouldn't wait,
He needed to find a young woman to mate.

His tribe had been sharply declining each year;
And Elders were worried they'd soon disappear.
With man-child exceeding the girls, four to one,
Some radical measures just had to be done.

Young men began trav'ling to lands far away,
In search of a young bride to bring home to stay.
With presents to woo them and give to their kin;
They hoped for a mate, then a girl child they'd win.

With warm clothing made from the sheepskins and wool,
He checked that his food packs were loaded and full.
Now ready to start his long trek to the north,
He steadied his bundles before setting forth.

He'd journeyed for many long days and harsh nights,
When snow started falling, obscuring his sight.
Although he was tired, he had to move on
If he fell asleep now, his life would be gone.

With darkness now coming, he couldn't delay;
But tired and weary he soon lost his way.
Despairingly knowing his journey was done.
He knew he was beaten; the mountain had won.

2000 AD

A party was climbing the mountain one day
All mindful of watching the ice melt away.
Their leader saw something and told them to wait
While he took a moment to investigate.

A part of the glacier had melted, to show
A body kept hidden just under the snow.
A man with a backpack who'd journeyed this way,
How long he'd been buried there, he couldn't say.

Our man on the mountain had been found at last,
And experts are able to study his past.
The gifts he'd been bearing, the clothes he had worn,
gave insights that otherwise never would dawn.

We hope that his spirit was able to rise,
and that he met someone up there in the skies.

~~oOo~~

A Forbidden Love ©

The lady holds her parasol and steps out in the sun,
with dainty shoes upon her feet and clothes stylishly spun.
Her tiny hands encased in tasteful gloves of Irish lace;
she walks along the promenade—a smile lights up her face.

***

The young man was stood waiting for the lady to arrive;
discretion is the only way for their love to survive.
A lady shouldn't be alone when she's out with a man,
but social difference means it is the only way she can.

***

He is a humble worker on her father's large estate,
and as a husband for his daughter he'd not tolerate.
Although their love for one another couldn't be denied—
until he could provide for her, their love they'd have to hide.

***

50

She saw him standing near the ice-cream parlour by the sea,
he turned, and when she saw him smile her heart leapt eagerly.
She passed him by and went around the corner out of sight,
and moments later she was being kissed to her delight.

***

Such times as these became the norm, they tried to meet each day
and steadfastly they swore that one day soon they'd run away.
He'd find a home for them somewhere her father wouldn't find,
where they could be together, but sometimes life is unkind.

***

One day when they were walking quietly beside the shore,
the lady felt her heart stop when she heard her father's roar.
He'd guessed something was going on, and followed close behind,
and now that he had caught them out, his anger turned his mind.

***

The reputation of the family had been destroyed,
through an illicit dalliance his daughter had enjoyed.
She'd shamed his name disgracefully; the rules had been ignored,
he would disown this daughter whom till now he had adored.

***

With no employment, her young man was forced to look around,
although, without a reference a job would not be found.
The lady had no home, and what she'd do she didn't know.
With no help from her so-called friends, she had no place to go.

***

The lady and her young man sat beside the ocean blue,
as neither knew where they could live, or even what to do.
It is a fact that scandal travels faster than the wind,
and they were cast aside by all convinced they both had sinned.

***

But sometimes news can reach someone who really doesn't care
of status or nobility, so long as love is there.
And in this case, it happened that a lady of renown
instructed her solicitor to track the couple down.

***

The search was on, it wasn't long—they found them just in time,
and brought them to the Duchess, who believed it was a crime
to banish these young people just because they were in love,
she said romance and couples go together hand in glove.

***

The lady, now companion to the Duchess, beams with joy
her young man's very happy to be also in employ.
The Duchess gave them 'happy ever after' as she said,
'God blessed your life, He blessed your love, He'll bless you as you
wed.'

~~oOo~~

How Far? ©

How far away is far away?
If someone knows, perhaps they'll say?
A thousand miles, a hundred yards,
just down the road, it can't be hard
to figure out what's very far
to walk to—or to use a car.

A telephone, that mighty arm,
can bring a smile, dispel alarm.
Yet seldom used to say hello
To let those lonely people know
They really do remember when
They used to visit now and then.

But now you live too far away…
How far is far? Would someone say?

~~oOo~~

Beguiled ©

She started off a poor wench
who would seek a better life,
so sought a rich and famous man,
and vowed to be his wife.

***

Her name was Anastasia,
her beauty was so rare,
her eyes were liquid pools of blue,
and starlight bathed her hair.

***

With skin of cream and dimples
on her cheeks each time she smiled,
It was no wonder that each man
she met became beguiled.

***

The King of Lancaster rode out
into the woods one day;
a kindly man and truly loved
by all who passed his way.

He spied the maiden as she sat
beneath the big oak tree--
her beauty so enchanted him,
he said, 'Pray, come with me.

***

I'll shower you with gold and pearls,
and gowns of finest silk,
and you can bathe in perfumed oils
all of the finest ilk.'

***

She coyly smiled and took his arm,
and promised she would stay
and be his queen from that day forth,
until his dying day.

***

He showered her with all his wealth,
and sat her on the throne,
until one day, to his dismay,
he heard the people moan.

***

With taxes raised to keep his bride,
he'd let his subjects down;
he said he'd give the money back or
abdicate his crown.

***

Queen Anastasia then tried
and failed to change his mind,
because the king had realised
this love had made him blind.

***

\>\>

He said she had bewitched him
and that now his eyes could see,
he'd lock her in the dungeon
and then throw away the key.

***

The queen had been prepared for this,
pretending now to cry,
she pricked him with her poisoned ring,
and then she watched him die.

***

Before the king took his last breath,
he opened up his eyes,
he smiled, and then he said these words,
much to the queen's surprise.

***

'You've only killed my body,
but my spirit is still strong,
I'll stay here till you go to hell,
which is where you belong.

***

The king had died still smiling,
and his spirit slipped away,
The queen would see him always,
he'd stay with her night and day.

***

No happy ever after comes
with this new fairy tale,
But if you listen you will hear
the queen's satanic wail.

~~oOo~~

In The Beginning©

A thousand words and more are penned,
before our lives come to an end--
Of joys and loves and pain and tears,
of feelings felt throughout those years.

We write of things that we can see
of things that should or should not be.
We write for good, decry the bad,
and write of joyful times, and sad.

We use our pens to show the plight
of innocents trapped in the night.
We take their cries to let all know
what happens where some fear to go.

And when our pens are put away
we know that someone else, one day,
will take the pledge to write the fight
and bring the darkness into light.

'In the beginning was the word'
This is God's gift--let it be heard.

~~oOo~~

Sweet Memories ©

One day when I went back to see
the house where I was born
It broke my heart to see it
standing so sad and forlorn.
This house that held such memories
for me and all my kin
Was calling now for me to go and take a look within.

***

I saw the house was up for sale
I went and got the keys
Then fought my way through weeds so high
and tall neglected trees.
The door creaked as it opened up
and took me back to when
my family all lived there, but were so much younger then.

***

I saw my brother standing there—
a grin upon his face
And dad was smiling next to mum,
it was a happy place.
Our family would soon increase
our mum would have two more,
My sister then another boy, this brother made it four.

***

Such times we had, but all too soon
we each of us left home
We all got wed and then we had
some children of our own.
As grandparents, our mum and dad,
they shone and loved us all.
I stand here with sweet memories as each one I recall.

***

I looked around and then I left,
those times are gone for good,
I'll take my memories with me,
this house told me I should.
And now it wants to start again,
make memories anew
Like these of mine, perhaps this house will make some just for you.

~~oOo~~

The Shawl ©

The little girl pulled close her threadbare shawl
And walked the trail up to the cattle shed.
Tonight, she knew, was special for them all;
She'd seen the star that shone bright overhead.

She heard the cattle low as she drew near,
But then a light much brighter than the day
Appeared and made the girl recoil in fear.
It was an Angel come to bar her way.

The frightened girl sank down upon her knees,
Her eyes shut tight as she began to pray.
In tears she cried to God, 'Forgive me, please,
It was the shining star brought me this way.'

'Do not be frightened, child,' the Angel said.
'God loves you so, and He is not displeased.
Tonight, within this lowly cattle shed,
God shows such love; He can't be disbelieved.'

The Angel smiled, then led her by the hand
Into the stable she where the girl could see
The son of God who now is born of man
To bring about a love eternally.

The little girl took off her shawl so worn
And said, "I have no gift that I can give,
Only my shawl that is so old and torn,
But it will keep Him warm enough to live."

Just then the baby boy gave her a smile.
It warmed her heart--her eyes lit up with joy.
His mother asked if she could stay a while
To help her wrap the shawl around the boy.

This sacred memory the girl would keep,
And as she left, some feathers filled her hand
While whispered words said, "Hold them as you sleep."
She smiled and left but didn't understand.

That night she prayed and then lay down her head.
She held the feathers tightly by her side,
And in the morning, folded on her bed,
She found a shawl so beautiful she cried.

~~oOo~~

A Wilted Flower ©

I often sit and wonder why
Love's passion always passed me by
While others sought and found the one
To share their love till life was done

I read in books, sweet poetry
Of love's keen glow and mystery
And how the heart can burst with joy
When shy young girl meets shy young boy

I often see love's radiance
On couples meeting just by chance
And hoped one day I too would meet
My true love walking down the street

But time has ticked by way too fast
I fear my chance of love has passed
A wilted flower gone to ground
My search for love was never found

And now I slowly wander home
Where I will sit there on my own
To read my books of poetry
Of love that has eluded me

~~~~

In This Field of Red ©

What was it that my mother saw that day so long ago,
when we stood in this field of red where only poppies grow?
I only know I was a child and didn't understand
when she told me, her father shed his blood upon this land.

I do remember watching as she wiped a tear away,
while telling me of brave young men who'd died for us that day.
Now only poppies bloom upon this land soaked with their blood,
reminding us of men who died in trenches full of mud.

It was a time so long ago, but I've come back once more
to think about those brave young men who perished on this shore.
They gave their lives believing there'd be no more tyranny;
that life would have no conflict in a world where all were free.

As I stand here in Flanders field, I know why Mother cried,
she saw the ghosts of soldiers who were asking why they died.

~~oOo~~

The Chimney Sweep Boy ©

When Toby sat up painfully
and struggled out of bed,
his tiny body ached so bad;
a drum beat in his head.

His tummy nagged him loudly
for some food but there was none,
a crust of bread is all he'd have
until this day was done.

His mother, in the scullery,
called out to her young lad,
'Just you make sure you're careful now,
don't make your mother sad.'

He weakly smiled and took his bread,
turned 'round, and then was gone.
At six years old he looked so thin;
how long could he go on?

Commencing work at five o'clock
the sky was still pitch black,
he hardly got to see daylight
while in the chimney stack.

Inside the flue he'd scrape and brush
the sticky soot away,
he never knew what childhood was—
he never got to play.

The work was harsh and tiring
and at times it was too tough,
their knees and elbows would be grazed
on bricks so coarse and rough.

If some boys were not quick enough,
their Master Sweeps won't wait,
to get them moving faster
they'd light fires in the grate.

Young Toby had been sweeping chimneys
since the age of five;
if he could reach the age of eight,
he'd leave the trade alive.

'Twas only yesterday he'd learnt
a friend of his had died,
when he'd got wedged he couldn't move,
no matter how he'd tried.

>>

When Toby went to work this day,
his body felt like lead,
he wished that he was back at home,
and fast asleep in bed.

His parents needed money—
every penny he would give,
which, added to his father's pay,
enabled them to live.

The Master Sweep was waiting
with his chimney sweeping gear,
he looked at Toby angrily
and grabbed him by the ear.

'You're late!' he bellowed harshly,
'so you'll lose an hour's pay.'
Though Toby knew he wasn't
he was too afraid to say.

'If you don't do yer job right,
then you'll get t' feel my fist!'
The Master Sweep then took him to
the first job on his list.

When Toby saw which house it was,
his heart sank like a stone,
too many boys had perished here
so frightened and alone.

With seven chimneys to be swept
young Toby made a start,
the first was easy, with no bends,
this was the central part.

The others curved and twisted,
filled with soot and other muck,
He knew what he must do
to ease the risk of getting stuck.

These chimneys were no longer safe
because they were so old,
though Toby felt quite dizzy now,
he'd do as he was told.

He climbed into the next one
where the bends closed off the light,
with little air now left to breathe,
he'd have to get this right.

He scraped and brushed the soot away
as further up he went,
around the corners, going up,
his breathing was soon spent.

At last he turned the corner
where he saw a speck of light,
but when he went to go ahead,
his body had jammed tight.

>>

He kicked his legs and breathed in hard
while pushing with his arms.
His shoulders stuck, he couldn't move,
and dread replaced alarm.

He thought about his family,
and then began to cry;
he screamed out loud, he was so scared,
without help he would die.

He pushed and pushed with all his strength,
but soon began to tire,
his nightmare would be coming true,
he knew they'd light the fire.

His throat felt raw, his eyes dried out,
his dizziness was bad;
as everything went 'round
he called out for his mum and dad.

Young Toby couldn't stay awake,
he knew he'd lost the fight,
he let his eyelids fall and close
as sleep removed his plight.

His body slumped and then
it was he saw his granny's face;
she took him by the hand and led him to a better place,

~~oOo~~

The Strange Encounter ©

The tension stretched between them seemed to sway,
as yellow eyes were focused on the man--
who stood so still he could not turn away,
while knowing he'd be foolish if he ran.

So, softly now, he hummed a soothing tune
that stirred the air between them with a sigh.
The wolf was list'ning keenly to him croon,
while standing proudly with his head held high.

The look he gave soon changed from fearsome scowl,
an ancient wisdom came into his eyes;
then suddenly the wolf began to howl,
the man was mesmerised with sheer surprise.

The wolf then yip yipped as he turned away...
and Man knew he would not forget this day.

~~oOO~~

Wedding Pearls

The calming touch of creamy pearls lay cool upon her hand,
Such elegance, a pure delight, made from a grain of sand.
Now passed on to the lady and then twisted through her hair
to compliment her wedding dress, and silken veil she'll wear.

The timeless beauty of the pearl, created over years,
is said to give the bearer many sad and troubled tears;
that if your husband gives them he is sure to make you cry,
but this is just another myth, another folklore lie.

The wearer of the pearl will have a strong relationship,
a caring, loyal person, with a smile upon the lips.
The marriage will be lasting, and each child will be adored,
the pearl conveys you're happy with your life and self-assured.

So if you're given pearls to wear upon your wedding day
don't listen to the pessimists, as love will guide the way.

Man Without a Name ©

'It was the strangest thing,' said Toby.
I was standing right there by his side,
    not one little word did he mutter—
he just turned around, sat down—and died!'
***
The policeman asked him more questions:
'Can you tell me how long he was there?
    Did he arrive first, or come later?
    Is there anything else you can share?'
***
'We arrived here around the same time.
    I remember he held an old hat.'
Toby stopped and turned for a moment.
'Look! It's still over there where he sat.'

***

The hat was picked up and examined;
    the detective was looking for clues.
'There's a name here—recently written—
it's the same name that's inside the shoes.'

***

Then Toby said, 'That could be handy.
With his name, you've got somewhere to go.'
The detective shook his head sadly.
'They are both too small for our John Doe.'
***

'Well, there must be someone who knows him.'
Toby frowned, thinking how it was sad.
'Perhaps he has people home waiting,
he just might be a husband and dad.'

***

When Toby went home, he was tired,
he could not get his mind off the man.
John Doe was no name to leave life with,
and his death - was it part of God's plan?
***

After Toby had climbed up the stairs,
he was soon fast asleep on his bed.
In dreams, John Doe came and was speaking;
he was stunned to hear what the man said.
***

'Please don't waste your time thinking of me;
life's too short as it is to do that.
There was nothing wrong with my passing—
I was destined to die where I sat.
***

'We each have our time to do something
for people to remember us by.
It is what you do that will matter;
there is no room for questioning why.'
***

Toby woke with the strangest feeling:
there was something he wanted to do.
The John Doe had clearly left something;
he'd unwittingly left them a clue.

***

He went first to ask the detective,
'Did you find the man who owned the hat?'
The detective said, 'Yes, we found him.
That's him there, as a matter of fact.'
***

Toby turned and saw an old drifter,
with a smart hat and shiny black shoes.
So he went and sat down beside him,
and the man said he'd heard the sad news.
***

The drifter was like many others,
who had come back from fighting the war.
Had nothing and nobody waiting;
he had lost the life he'd had before.
***

Discharged from the army a hero
he'd been wounded, and lost his right arm.
He was forced to live like a drifter,
but he'd never do anyone harm.
***

'One day, this man came and sat with me
he saw that my shoes were too tight,
so he took off his own and his hat,
and he told me it just wasn't right.'
***

He then swapped his things for the drifter's,
though the shoes were too tight for him, too.
The drifter looked up with a question,
'Wasn't that a real strange thing to do?'
***

Toby thought of the dream he'd had then,
and he smiled at the drifter and said,
'I am sure you'll remember the man,
but not as a John Doe who is dead.'

~~oOo~~

The Little Girl ©

An uproar in the village had the neighbours' running out,
'My little boy is missing!' They all heard the mother shout.
The police came with their sniffer dogs for searching all around;
though everyone was fearful, they all hoped he would be found.

'They didn't lock their door, they said, in fact, it was ajar.
The girl just wandered in with him, he hadn't gone too far.'
The news reporter took some notes, then asked him to go on.
'Just tell me everything you know before the girl was gone.'

When Mr Peal sat down upon the sofa by the door,
he sighed and said, 'It really was a miracle, for sure.
Who was this child, this little girl?
There's some who think they know,
from stories that their parents told, so many years ago.'

The news reporter stayed his pen; was this another hoax?
He'd had enough of idiots just playing silly jokes.
'Now, hold on please,' said Mr Peal, 'and hear the story out.
You need to know before you go just how it came about.'

The news reporter settled back, deciding he would stay.
'Okay, I am all ears,' he said. 'I'll hear what you've to say.'
Then Mr Peal took out some pictures
from his open case,
he put them on the table and sat back to watch his face.

'Where did you get these photos from?' the news reporter pried.
He touched them gently--turning them to see the other side.
'Are these authentic pictures? Are you certain they are real?'
He took another look to see what else they would reveal.

'What do you see?' asked Mr Peal; a smile played on his lips.
The news reporter traced the pictures with his fingertips.
'I see something impossible,
yet here before my eyes,
are images that are alike; which is a big surprise.'

At last, he saw his curiosity had been disturbed,
so Mr Peal pulled out more pictures feeling unperturbed.
'These photos here we know were taken eighty years ago,
while these were printed yesterday. This much is what we know.'

'The child is in both pictures but then how did that occur?
She looks the same, the house is too, I can't deny it's her.'
The news reporter looked up
as the question lingered there.
'So, tell me, what's the story? Will it be one I can share?'

'This story started long ago; if you decide to tell,
make sure you get the facts down and you write the story well.
This little girl was born way back in nineteen-forty-four;
the war was coming to an end, and hope began to soar.

Her parents bought this little house; their futures looking bright,
they made a home and then their baby girl made it feel right.
When Jessica was four years old,
her brother came along;
and that, my friend, became the start when everything went wrong.

Her father was a baker, it was work that he enjoyed;
the job was one he'd trained for; he was glad to be employed.
The owner was a friend of his, and once peace was declared,
the job was there, he'd qualified, and so he was prepared.

One day, when he was kneading dough, he heard a slamming door;
he went to take a look and saw his boss laid on the floor.
A heart attack, they told him,
he was dead before he fell;
they closed the shop and let him know his job had gone as well.

He only had one option left--he must work down the mine;
as much as he disliked it, it would pay their bills on time.
The mine in which her father worked caved in one rainy day--
though many died and some survived, so few would walk away.

As both of Jessie's father's legs were crushed beyond repair,
her mother took in washing and whatever work was there.
With no one else to help them,
Jessica was asked to do
some work around the house and mind her little brother too.

As all the laughter left their home, and sadness came to stay,
young Jessica would do her best; it left no time for play.
It happened one day while at home with just her brother there,
when Jessie turned around she couldn't find him anywhere.

She searched the rooms then ran outside, and loudly called his name;
her body shook so badly as she screamed until help came.
The police arrived, her neighbours' too,
and then her mum was there,
and Jessie cried so wretchedly, such was the child's despair.

They never found that little boy and Jessie blamed herself,
and then her mother found the note she'd left there on the shelf.
Because she thought they blamed her, Jessie lost the will to live.
She hoped one day her parents would be able to forgive.'

The news reporter sat there silently for quite a while;
he picked the photo up again and traced her happy smile.
'So you believe the young girl
who had been around that day,
was this poor little Jessica? Is that what people say?'

'It does make sense,' said Mr Peal. 'She led that boy back home.
Just like her little brother, he had walked off on his own.
I'd like to think that this has helped her cut her earthly chain
and that she's now in Heaven with her family again.'

~~oOo~~

The Great Fire of London ©

It was sixteen sixty-six, the second of September,
the hottest, driest year many folk could well remember;
most London streets were narrow—
wooden buildings hot as hell.
With everything so tinder dry, the signs did not bode well.

As Pudding Lane was settling down, the trading places shut,
it was the time for merriment, for men to prance and strut;
while females flounce and flaunt their wares
to do just what they can,
to get themselves a night of fun with any wealthy man.

When Thomas, the King's baker, went to close up for the night,
He turned and bade his maid douse all the stoves and snuff the light.
Though Mary was exhausted
working fifteen hours a day,
She knew she would soon be in bed to sleep the night away.

She'd closed her eyes a second...or perhaps a moment more,
when she heard a crackling sound;
then smoke come through the door.
As Mary scampered from her blanket, flames leapt on her bed,
With nothing there to put it out, the blaze climbed overhead.

Extremely frightened, realising just what she had done,
That being tired would not save her from her master's tongue.
One oven must have been left burning,
spitting sparks about,
And then she saw with cold conviction--she had no way out!

She tried to squeeze out through the window, but it was too small,
By then the burning beams above her, all began to fall.
The baker's shop in Pudding Lane
was Mary's funeral pyre,
As she became the first to die in London's greatest fire.

The fire started spreading out more buildings were aflame.
From house to house the blaze extended; churches burned the same.
The flames had gained momentum,
and they feared the city lost,
But then King Charles demanded it be stopped at any cost.

He ordered buildings be destroyed, to make a firebreak,
And gave instructions what to do;
their future was at stake.
With gunpowder, a row of homes was quickly taken out,
Along with other buildings that were standing round about.

With nothing left to fuel the fire the flames soon died away,
And Londoners who'd lost their homes looked for a place to stay.
From lessons learnt, they passed new laws,
and new rules were applied,
and everyone was thankful less than ten people had died.

~~oOo~~

Brave Joe ©

When Rachel ran down to the water
with her brother Joe,
she wondered if it would be warm
and dipped in with her toe.

It was so cold, but little Joe cared less and ran on in,
then Rachel watched him in the shallow,
practicing to swim.

He laughed and splashed and called to her,
but Rachel shook her head;
she told him it was much too cold
and she'd sit down instead.

When, in a while, young Joe came out, he very nearly fell;
as Rachel ran and caught him,
he said, 'I don't feel too well.'

When they reached home, their mother
quickly packed him off to bed,
then went and got a wet,
cold flannel to put on his head.

'We'll let him sleep, now don't you fret.'
She gave Rachel a hug.
'It's just a chill, there's loads about,
there's many catch the bug.'

When Joe woke up next morning,
he tried getting out of bed;
he aimed to stand upon his feet
but then fell down instead.

He screamed out for his mum and dad;
they ran in through the door.
'I can't stand up.' He looked so scared,
laid down there on the floor.

While Dad put Joe back into bed,
Mum called the doctor out.
The doctor came, and then he said,
'There's polio about.

He'll have to go to hospital...go in an iron lung.'
They looked at Joe, just six years old,
a nightmare had begun.

It was to be a year before
Joe came back home again;
a year of tears and suffering,
and lots of mental pain.

With legs in braces always now
and crutches to lean on,
those happy days he'd shared before
were now forever gone.

His sister felt she was to blame
for what Joe had gone through,
and tried to help him do the things
she knew he'd like to do.

>>

She took him to the park,
but there he saw the other boys
all playing football, doing things that every kid enjoys.

Then Rachel gave up everything
to help her brother Joe;
she worked the muscles in his legs,
just hoping they would grow.

Although her parents told her
that she hadn't been to blame,
she felt she was as she'd been there;
now Joe was not the same.

The years went by and Joe grew up;
his braces were removed,
and though he'd always need a stick,
his muscles had improved.

With Rachel's help, he'd lived a life
much better than he'd thought,
he felt that he'd been luckier
than others who'd been caught.

Although his withered legs had never
grown the way they should;
with his devoted sister's help, they were still pretty good.

New Beginnings. ©

I wander through the wilderness of night,
where winds have blown the open meadows bleak;
and limbs of trees are bent and cowed with fright,
while hiding from the force that blizzards wreak.

The sun, now spent, has long thrown off its rays,
and clouds, once warm, now cooled by frosts that bite.
Too soon I'll feel the chill of winter days,
then watch as snow turns chequered fields to white.

I wander on through fields of broken corn,
once planted for the food we hoped they'd yield.
But nature wasn't kind and farmers mourn;
no hallowed harvest gleaned from ruined field.

I long have been acquainted by the might
of Mother Nature's moods throughout the year.
The way she can destroy, then put things right,
and warm the land to bring about some cheer.

I wander through the wilderness of night,
The sun, now spent, has long thrown off its rays.
Yet, if I look I'll see in morning's light,
the start of new beginnings on the way.

~~oOo~~

Nursed on Jesus' Knee ©

I watched her as she sat beside
the fountain in the square,
although not young, I saw she had
a timeless, graceful air;

her silver curls fell softly
'round a face calm and serene
and in her eyes, I saw a gentleness
I'd never seen.

I sat beside her on the bench,
she smiled and said 'hello.'
We talked about the weather...
watched the birds fly to and fro.

As children came to put their fingers
in the fountain's spray,
the lady smiled and I could see
she loved to watch them play.

'I had a baby girl," she said.
Her voice seemed far away...
"But even though I loved her,
she was not allowed to stay.'

She turned and looked into my eyes,
I held my breath...she sighed.
"The angels came to talk to me
the night my baby died.

"My little baby daughter
was an angel sent to me,
God wanted me to know
that it was how it had to be.

She had to share her spirit
for a moment here on Earth,
And that is why I lost my child
so soon after her birth.

"The angels promised me that
she would be there when I go,
she'd meet me when my soul returned.
They wanted me to know.

I told them I would like my baby
to be Christened Pearl,
because they were so rare and precious,
like my baby girl.

'That same night when they took her back,
I was allowed to see,
my cherished baby daughter
being nursed on Jesus' knee.'

I sat there very quietly; I couldn't understand
Why she had to suffer, I reached out and held her hand.

Winding Paths

Your path can be as straight in life
as you'd like it to be
It can go on in one long path into infinity

As tall as trees that fight the breeze
to stand and never bend
you'll live your life with blinkered eyes
right up until the end

But if your path has winding trails
that bid you walk along
you might find there are tunes
that play another kind of song

that open up your mind
to many possibilities
to see such sights that you might miss
like trees that bend with ease

Just take that chance to twirl and dance
and set your spirit free
Go find yourself a new romance
with life as it should be

Butterflies (A Pleiades)

Butterflies dance on air
Boasting their grace and flair
Bystanders stop and stare
Beauty beyond compare
Buddleia plants that wear
Blue and white flowers fair
Bring the butterflies there

~~oOo~~

They Took it all Away

He was a man of pride,
he had a home and family,
a wife, he loved, and children,
everything as it should be.

He loved his job, he did it well,
he couldn't want for more,
until that day when his world crashed
and life fell through the floor.

The management called everyone
to meet that dreadful day,
and all were told the company was closed;
they could not pay

their wages now, as shares had crashed,
their pensions had gone too.
The management were sorry—
there was nothing they could do.

Without his wages coming in,
and no work there to find,
his home was repossessed
and suddenly life was unkind.

His wife left with the children
as he hit an all-time low,
she went back to her parents—
she had no place else to go.

As time went by, with hope all gone,
his home was in the park,
his bed was just an old hard bench,
he'd go there after dark.

On sunny days, the nights were warm,
but winter would arrive
and chill him to the bone;
he knew he never would survive.

One night when he was fast asleep,
the snow began to fall,
and in his frozen mind he thought
he heard an angel call.

He felt a hand slip into his,
and someone call his name,
his eyelids fluttered open as
he heard the voice again.

And there she stood, with gentle smile
that brought him from the brink,
she helped him up and took him where
they gave him food and drink.

She gave him back his dignity,
she took away his pain--
she brought him back to life,
and then she helped him start again.

The man who fell asleep that night
beneath a freezing sky,
Is testament to kindness;
she refused to let him die.

~~oOo~~

I Knew I'd Always Love you ©

I knew I'd always love you
from that moment you were born,
With hair so soft and silky,
and your eyes bright as the dawn.

Your skin so smooth, your nose so cute,
your lovely lips so sweet,
Ten tiny fingers on your hands,
and ten toes on your feet.

You stole my heart that moment
when they put you in my arms,
I swore to God right there and then,
I'd keep you safe from harm.

That little smile you always gave me
when you caught my eye,
When you came home from school each day,
that smile lit up my sky.

As years went by you went from child,
and grew to be a man,
And on your way you'd always strive
to do the best you can.

I knew I'd always love you
from that moment you were born,
And swore to God I'd keep you safe
from troubles that might dawn.

Then came the day I'm standing proud,
a husband you will be,
A lovely wife stood by your side,
your own sweet family.

One day you came to see me with
a twinkle in your eye,
I was to be a grandmother
and I began to cry!

When first I saw her silky hair,
her eyes bright as the dawn-
I knew I'd always love her
from that moment she was born.

~~oOo~~

If I Could Turn Back Time

If we could turn back time again and have a second go--
but taking with us things we did and all we came to know,
I wonder what we'd change about the lives we live today;
would we still walk the route we took, or go a different way?

How many times I've wanted to take back a spoken word,
or wished that what I'd said aloud had not been overheard.
How many times I wished I'd told someone how much I cared;
but time rushed by, and too late now, those feelings can't be shared.

Sometimes I get so cross with time, it never takes a breath;
it marches on relentlessly, from birth until our death.
We can't go back, it is a fact, we cannot change the past.
There's nothing else quite like it; time's a factor made to last.

But, if I could, I know I would repeat some things I've done--
enjoy the life I lived with both my parents and my sons.
The love I've shared, with nothing spared, was worth the time apart,
for what I had with them will always live within my heart.

~~oOo~~

Sweet Puppy Angel
By Sandra Stoner Mitchell

Sweet Puppy Angel, tell me what you dream,
while sleeping on your cloud beneath the sun.
You could be playing by a trickling stream,
Or are you chasing cats you can't outrun?

Sweet Puppy Angel, I can see your wings,
they quiver as you dream of frisky days.
while you're asleep, you might be catching rings,
that in your dreams I'm sure are thrown your way.

Sweet Puppy Angel, would you like to race
in fields of daisies freshly sprayed with dew?
Or could there be another secret place,
that in your dreams is only known by you?

While you are sleeping, I just muse and sigh.
Sweet Puppy Angel, dreaming in the sky.

~~oOo~~

A Special Poem For my Mum

But....

I can't put into words the way I feel
when Mother's Day arrives and you're not here.
I see the happy faces
in the parks and other places—but…
without you Mum—I'm left to shed a tear
~O~
Remember all the fun times that we had?
We'd laugh at silly things until we cried.
No one else could take your place;
oh, how I miss your smiling face—but…
my heart has memories of you inside
~O~
Although no longer here, you're still my mum
You loved me more than anyone I've known.
While you were the very best,
God said it's time for you to rest—but…
sometimes I feel so lost and all alone.
~O~
I love you very much, I'll have you know—but…
God called your name and you just had to go.

A Special Poem for my Dad

Why?...

We didn't realise your name was called
That awful day we had to say 'goodbye'
You fell asleep as we stood near
Mum held your hand and shed a tear
And all I did was stand and question … Why?

I took Mum home … she didn't understand
Why you were taken and neither did I
We called your name and felt the pain
That filled our hearts … and then again
I held Mum close as we both questioned … Why?

I hope you knew how much I love you, Dad
Now Mum is with you I'm just left to cry
She couldn't live without you near
She loved you so but you weren't here
I've lost you both and still I question … Why?

Now you are both together, I can't hide
How pleased I am you're by each other's side.

~~oOo~~

Thank you for reading my poems. If you like this book, and have the time to put a review on Amazon, I would be happy to read your thoughts.

Poetry comes from deep inside your heart
Your mind and your soul

Emotions that lie beneath thought
but sentiments that belong to you

Allow them to flow.

By the same author

Children's Books

Hedgerow Capers
The Day Before Christmas Eve
A Spot of Bother
The Fun Begins

Amazing Animal AlphaRhymes
Casper The Caterpillar
The Tooth Fairy
The Witch and the Fairy

Novels

This Time – That Time Bk 1
Beyond That Time Bk 2

Your own favourite

Add a poem that is your all-time favourite

Sandra Stoner-Mitchell was born in Ipswich, Suffolk, England. Moving to Gillingham in Kent at the age of six years old. When she was twelve years old, her parents made their final move to Southampton in Hampshire.

Married and widowed by the age of thirty-nine, she brought up her two sons on her own. Sandra later found love again and married Graham. They later moved to Spain and lived there for eleven happy years, but moved back to England to be with her family again.

It was during her time in Spain that Sandra began writing seriously, and had her first rhymed children's story book, Hedgerow Capers, published, followed by five more.

In 2016, Sandra had her first novel published, This Time-That Time, the first book in a trilogy of time travel.

This book is a collection of poems Sandra has written for contests over the years. Many of them but also had honorable mentions for others. Another book of her poems will be published later in the year.

10302450R00056

Printed in Great Britain
by Amazon